TAYLOR
LAUTNER

TWILIGHT'S FEARLESS WEREWOLF

ELAINE LANDAU

For Michael Brent Pearl,
our handsome Taylor Lautner
look-alike!

Lerner Publications Company
A division of Lerner Publishing Group, Inc.
241 First Avenue North
Minneapolis, MN 55401 U.S.A.

Website address: www.lernerbooks.com

Library of Congress Cataloging-in-Publication Data

Landau, Elaine.
    Taylor Lautner : Twilight's fearless werewolf / by Elaine Landau.
        p.   cm. — (Pop culture bios: action movie stars)
    Includes index.
    ISBN 978-1-4677-0745-9 (lib. bdg. : alk. paper)
        1. Lautner, Taylor, 1992– —Juvenile literature.
    2. Actors—United States—Biography—Juvenile literature.   I. Title.
PN2287.L2855L36   2013
791.4302'8092—dc23 [B]   2012018296

Manufactured in the United States of America
1 – PC – 12/31/12

ABDO

Green goo covers hottie Taylor Lautner after he was slimed at the 2012 Kids' Choice Awards.

It's the night of March 31, 2012. Millions of young people can't be pried away from their TV sets. The 25th annual Kids' Choice Awards are on. Twilight Saga cutie Taylor Lautner is a main attraction.

What award is Taylor up for? It isn't a favorite actor award or even a prize for Hollywood's hottest hunk. No, this adorable star has been nominated in the category of Favorite Buttkicker! The Favorite Buttkicker prize goes to the celeb who kids think shows the most bravery and toughness.

There's no doubt that Taylor is tough. In the Twilight Saga, his character goes to great lengths to protect his friend Bella from dangerous vampires. Still, Taylor has some stiff competition. He's up against Jessica Alba from *Spy Kids: All the Time in the World in 4D*, Tom Cruise of the Mission: Impossible series, and Kelly Kelly of WWE fame. Will he pull off a win?

Taylor hangs out at the 2012 Kids' Choice Awards.

Viewers get their answer when hosts Miranda Cosgrove and Robert Downey Jr. invite Taylor up to the stage. They announce that fans have indeed chosen him as their Favorite Buttkicker! Taylor graciously accepts his award. "This whole awards show is about the kids," he says after claiming his prize. "I'm so thankful to have all of them behind us."

The excitement's far from over once Taylor has his prize in hand. Every year at the KCAs, some celebs get slimed. A good amount of green gunk rains down on them. It's usually fan favorites who get doused the most with goo—so

bert Downey Jr. (RIGHT) and Miranda Cosgrove hand Taylor the award for Favorite Buttkicker.

you can bet that Taylor Lautner is in trouble!

Does Taylor get annoyed as the sticky green slime soaks him? No way. He laughs all through the sliming. Of course, Taylor has good reason to grin. He's an actor loved by millions. He's got awesome looks and talent. Want to know more about Taylor? Keep reading. Soon you'll know all there is to know about this dazzling star who really does kick butt.

ER ONE

HIGAN BOY

Taylor shows off his killer karate moves in 2005.

Taylor Daniel Lautner came into the world on February 11, 1992, in Grand Rapids, Michigan. His mom, Deborah Lautner, is a computer software developer. His dad, Daniel Lautner, is an airline pilot. Taylor was an only child for about six years. Then his little sister, Makena, joined the family. The pair was brought up in Hudsonville, Michigan, a small town just outside Grand Rapids. They were raised to be respectful and well-mannered.

From the time he was small, Taylor had tons of energy. His parents also noticed that he had natural coordination. They thought karate might be a good fit with his abilities. They signed him up for lessons when he was six. Taylor's coach quickly saw that he was *great* at karate!

Taylor poses with his sister, Makena, in 2005.

By the age of eight, Taylor had already earned his black belt. And that was just the start of his karate career. In a few short years, he became a three-time Junior World Champion.

BLACK BELT = a black sash, or belt, that a person wears in karate after reaching the highest level in the sport

Not Just a Jock

Taylor's coach admired his student's performance in competitions.

Taylor's karate coach saw that Taylor wasn't afraid to be the center of attention.

In particular, he noticed how naturally Taylor moved in the ring. He also saw that Taylor was supercomfortable with being the center of attention. Taylor didn't have any of the nervousness that most karate students have when they demonstrate their skills for a crowd.

Taylor's coach remarked to his parents that their son might make a good actor. Taylor's parents took the comment very seriously! They signed Taylor up with a talent agency in Los Angeles, California.

Taylor walks with his father, Daniel.

TALENT AGENCY =
a business that sets up tryouts for people who want to act

...ylor and his family lived in this house after they moved to California.

CHAPTER TWO

CALIFORNIA, WHERE HE COMES!

When Taylor first signed on with the agency, he and his parents would fly from Michigan to Los Angeles for auditions. But by the time Taylor was ten, his parents decided to make things easier for the family. They moved to Santa Clarita, California. This brought Taylor closer to the film industry. It would be easier for him to try out for parts in movies and commercials.

Meanwhile, Taylor did other things to improve his performing skills. He took hip-hop and jazz dance classes. These gave him grace and made him even more comfortable with being onstage. He also played school sports.

AUDITIONS =
tryouts for TV and movie roles

IF AT FIRST YOU DON'T SUCCEED, TRY, TRY AGAIN

Taylor Lautner's first audition was for a Burger King commercial. That day, he didn't have it his way. Taylor didn't get the part. But he never gave up!

Besides keeping him fit—which was important to Taylor, since acting can be physically demanding—the sports were just plain fun for him. He especially enjoyed football and basketball.

Dream Life?

Taylor seemed to be living a dream life. But was he really? He had to balance small acting jobs with schoolwork and sports. That wasn't easy. And not everyone at school thought acting was cool. Some kids bullied Taylor about his acting. "I just had to tell myself, *I can't let this get*

ALL WORK AND NO PLAY? NO WAY!

As a teen, Taylor did his share of dating. Even before he was a star, girls were crazy about him! His high school GF was Sara Hicks. The two dated seriously for almost a year in 2006 and 2007.

to me," Taylor said of the bullying. *"This is what I love to do."* Still, the bullying made Taylor's life hard. Of course, these days, no one remembers those bullies—but everyone knows who Taylor Lautner is!

Tryout after Tryout

Taylor went on tons of auditions after moving to California. But he didn't get a starring role in a movie for years. Between 2001 and 2005, he had small roles on a number of TV shows, including *The Bernie Mac Show* and *My Wife and Kids*. He also had a tiny part in the film *Cheaper by the Dozen 2*.

Taylor (FAR RIGHT) acts in *Cheaper by the Dozen 2* in 2005.

In addition, Taylor took voice-over roles. He had voice-over roles in two TV series—*What's New, Scooby-Doo?* and *Danny Phantom.*

His First Starring Role

Taylor kept his eyes on the prize as he took on small parts. He kept on trying for a starring part in a major film. At last, it happened for him. In 2005, he landed his first starring role. Taylor played Sharkboy in *The Adventures of Sharkboy and Lavagirl 3-D.* Sharkboy is a superhero from

Taylor easily landed the lead role in *The Adventures of Sharkboy and Lavagirl 3-D.*

Taylor and castmates Taylor Dooley (CENTER) and Cayden Boyd hang at the premiere of *The Adventures of Sharkboy and Lavagirl 3-D.*

Planet Drool. In the film, Taylor has fins, sharp teeth, and pointy claws. Taylor's karate skills came in handy in the movie's fighting scenes. Taylor was the very first young actor to try out for the part. His talent wowed those casting for the movie. He was chosen for the role right away!

HIT OR MISS?

Did film critics love *The Adventures of Sharkboy and Lavagirl 3-D?* No. In fact, they hated it! But the film was not an epic fail for Taylor. It got him his first award nomination. He was nominated for Best Performance in a Feature Film at the 2006 Young Artist Awards. Taylor didn't win. But just being nominated put his name on the map.

CHAPTER THREE

TAYLOR'S BIG BREAK

Taylor is all smiles at the Twilight premiere in 2009 with costars Kristen Stewart (CENTER) and Robert Pattinson (RIGHT).

jacob

twilight

Taylor was plenty excited about the part he played in *The Adventures of Sharkboy and Lavagirl 3-D*. But something bigger—*much* bigger!—soon came his way. In 2008, Taylor got a call from his talent agency. The agency told him that they'd signed him up to audition for a part in the action-romance film saga Twilight. "My [agency] told me, 'Yeah, this one's kind of big. This one's big,'" Taylor recalled. "And I was like, 'I've never heard of it.'"

That's right—Taylor had never heard of the Twilight Saga! The Twilight books, published between 2005 and 2008 and made into five films, have a huge fan following. But the literary craze had passed Taylor right by. Still, he was excited to find out all he could about Twilight, and he couldn't wait for his audition.

Taylor with Twilight author Stephenie Meyer.

Taylor with *Twilight* director Catherine Hardwicke in 2009.

When the day of the audition came, Taylor read lines from the script for director Catherine Hardwicke. Then he had an agonizing wait. One month later, he learned that he was among the top three candidates being considered for the part of Jacob Black! If Taylor got the part, the entire world would know him as the handsome half human, half wolf BFF of main character Bella Swan. Taylor was ecstatic.

Just a short time later, Taylor got even better news. He'd been chosen to play Jacob! He couldn't believe his luck. He devoured all four Twilight books to help him get ready for the role (and he *loved* them). He also spent tons of time studying his lines and rehearsing his part with fellow cast members.

TAYLOR'S IDOLS

Which actors does Taylor Lautner admire? Two of his favs are Tom Cruise (RIGHT)—a fellow Favorite Buttkicker nominee—and Matt Damon. He's loved these actors' movies since he was just a little kid.

Taylor (RIGHT) in Twilight alongside Kristen Stewart (LEFT), Billy Burke (TOP CENTER), and Gil Birmingham (BOTTOM CENTER).

Giant Hits

When *Twilight* came to theaters, it was a giant box office hit. People stood in line for hours to see it. Taylor turned into a teen idol. He also became superrich. In 2010, Lautner was said to be the highest-paid teen actor in Hollywood. Taylor enjoyed the fame and wealth. But his favorite part of the Twilight Saga was just being part of the phenomenon.

twilight

THE #1 *NEW YORK TIMES* BESTSELLER BY
STEPHENIE MEYER

TWI-MOMS

Taylor's fans are not just tweens and teens. Twi-Moms are mothers and even grandmothers who love the Twilight Saga and its stars. Taylor's fans range in age from eight to eighty!

Taylor gets up close with excited fans at the *Twilight* World Premiere in 2008.

"Twilight is really unlike anything else," Taylor reflected on the part he played in the films. "I know that over the past couple of years, I've had the time of my life."

Bulking Up

Taylor really had to bulk up for his role in *New Moon*—the second Twilight Saga film. He put on 30 pounds (14 kilograms) of muscle. Taylor did a lot of weight training. He also had to eat much more. "At one point, I had to shove as much food in my body as possible," Taylor spilled. "My trainer wanted me to do six meals a day and not go two hours without eating."

After *New Moon*, Taylor became even more popular. Yet fame didn't really change him. He still lives at home with his family. He keeps in touch with many of his old friends too.

Taylor held the number two slot on *Glamour* magazine's "50 Sexiest Men of 2010" list. The same year, he ranked fourth on *People*'s "Most Amazing Bodies" list. Looks like all his bulking up paid off!

"Jacob's angry werewolf side is not like me in real life," Taylor dished. "I'm very friendly, outgoing, energetic, and easy to talk to." Both guys and girls like Taylor Lautner. And it's no wonder! He's one of those people you just can't help but feel drawn to.

Taylor's rockin' bod r
its debut in *New M*

HE FUTURE

Taylor in
Abduction in 2011

ylor does his own stunts
the filming of *Abduction*.

Taylor became a star through the Twilight Saga movies—but his success continued after the filming was over. The young celeb looked for new roles in different types of films. He wanted to grow as an actor.

In 2011, Taylor found a great new project to step into as Twilight ended. It was an exciting action film called *Abduction*. Taylor got to use his karate skills in the movie. He also learned new skills for his role, including boxing, motorcycle riding, and wrestling. "I had to do about three months of training," he said of the prep work for *Abduction*. "[It] was a lot of fun. I really enjoyed the boxing. It was a great workout."

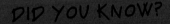

DID YOU KNOW?

Taylor may look like a "guy's guy," but he's totes in love with his tiny Maltese dog! The furry white fluff ball is named Roxy.

Some Very Special Girls

In addition to keeping busy with work, Taylor had a lot going on in his personal life. In 2011, he was linked to actress Lily Collins, his costar in *Abduction*. The two dated for a while. Their relationship ended shortly before *Abduction* was released, but Taylor still has many good things to say about Lily. "She was great [in *Abduction*]," Taylor

Taylor and Sara Hicks in 2012

Taylor and Lily Collins in 2011

OTHER PASTIMES

In addition to hanging with GFs and friends, Taylor likes following sports in his free time. His favorite sport to watch is football. He especially admires NFL players Brett Favre, Tom Brady, and Jerry Rice.

enthused. "I'm so excited for people to see her in this movie." Taylor also went out with his high school girlfriend Sara Hicks again. The pair seems to be rekindling the romance they had back in high school. But only time will tell if Taylor and Sara will wind up together in the end.

What's Ahead?

No one can see into the future, but most people think Taylor's future will be bright. He's shown himself to be a talented actor. He also has scores of loyal fans. Plus, he works hard to live a balanced life. "I still have the same life that I've always had," Taylor says on maintaining a work-life balance. "I go home and see my family and hang out with my friends. I play football and help out around the house. I think that is really important." Taylor seems to handle stardom well. That's a good thing, since it looks like Taylor's star will be shining brightly for many years to come!

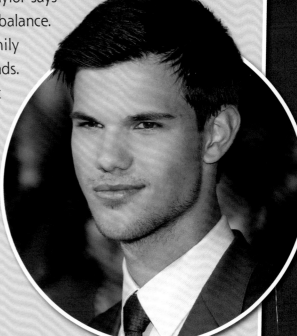

TAYLOR
PICS!

GRAUMAN'S CHINESE THEATER

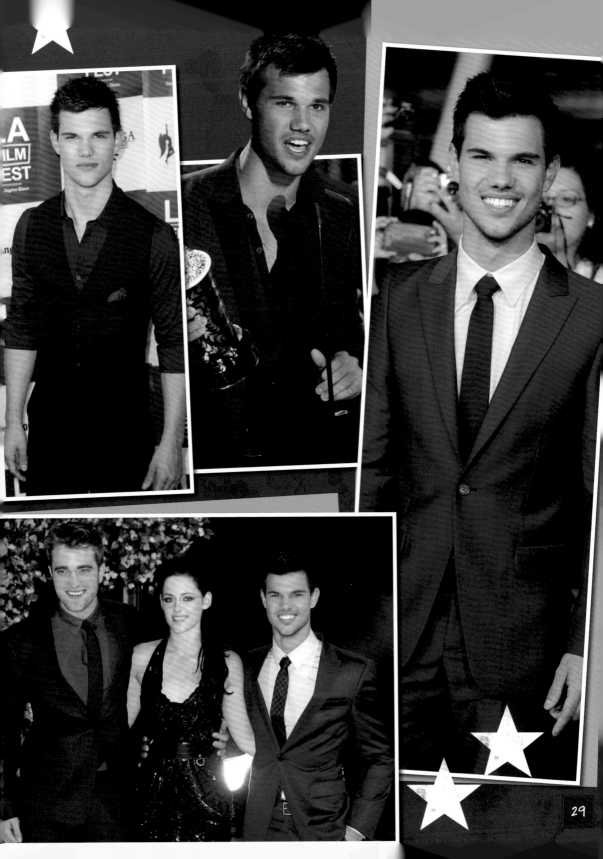

SOURCE NOTES

6   "Taylor Lautner Won Best Buttkicker!," YouTube video, .7, posted by
      iluvgreenPRODUCTION1, March 31, 2012, http://www.youtube.com
      /watch?v=UUXnrnCzkRc (May 16, 2012).

14–15 GlamourVanity, "Taylor Lautner," GV.com, n.d., http://www.glamourvanity.com/taylor-
      lautner/ (May 18, 2012).

19   Rebecca Murray, "Exclusive Interview with Taylor Lautner," About.com, n.d., http:
      //movies.about.com/od/twilight/a/taylor-lautner.htm (May 18, 2012).

22   IMDb.com, "Biography for Taylor Lautner," Internet Movie Database, 2012, http://www
      .imdb.com/name/nm1210124/bio (May 21, 2012).

22   Who's Dated Who, "Taylor Lautner Quotes," Whosdatedwho.com, 2012, http://www
      .whosdatedwho.com/tpx_46646/taylor-lautner/quotes (May 21, 2012).

23   Ibid.

25   Christina Radish, "Taylor Lautner Talks about Abduction and The Twilight Saga: Breaking
      Dawn," Collider.com, September 16, 2011, http://collider.com/taylor-lautner-abduction-
      twilight-breaking-dawn-interview/115419/ (May 21, 2012).

26   Ibid.

27   Ibid.

MORE TAYLOR INFO

Azzarelli, Ally. Taylor Lautner: Film Superstar. Berkeley Heights, NJ: Enslow Publishers, 2011.
Superstar Taylor Lautner comes to life in this interesting bio. You'll learn about his childhood, the
girls he's dated, and his plans for the future. The personal stories and timeline are fun features too.

IMDb: Taylor Lautner
http://www.imdb.com/name/nm1210124
Check out this site for a bio of Taylor, official pics of the star, and a complete list of the movies he's
been in.

Lusted, Marcia Amidon. Booboo Stewart: Twilight's Breakout Idol. Minneapolis: Lerner Publications
Company, 2013. Learn more about the Twilight phenomenon and one of its breakout stars, the
adorable Booboo Stewart!

Murphy, Maggie. Taylor Lautner. New York: PowerKids Press, 2011. This bio traces Taylor Lautner's
career from start to stardom.

Nelson, Robin. Taylor Swift: Country Pop Hit Maker. Minneapolis: Lerner Publications Company,
2013. Read all about the fascinating career of onetime Taylor Lautner GF Taylor Swift—a highly
talented performer in her own right.

Taylor Lautner Fan
http://www.taylor-lautner.net
Are you a true Taylor Lautner fan? Then be sure not to miss this website. It has breaking news on
Taylor's upcoming movies and appearances. It's packed with fab photos too!

Williams, Mel. Taylor Lautner: Overnight Sizzlin' Sensation. New York: Simon Pulse, 2009. Want to
know more about how Taylor Lautner got his start? If so, don't miss this book. You'll learn all
about his hometown roots and his love of extreme sports.

INDEX

PHOTO ACKNOWLEDGMENTS

The images in this book are used with the permission of: © Christopher Polk/KCA2012/Getty Images, pp. 2, 4 (both), 5; © Lester Cohen/WireImage/Getty Images, pp. 3 (top), 22; © s_buckley/Shutterstock.com, pp. 3 (bottom), 24 (bottom right); AP Photo/Chris Pizzello, p. 6; © Jeff Kravtiz/FilmMagic/Getty Images, p. 7; © Albert L. Ortega/WireImage/Getty Images, p. 8 (top); © Katy Winn/CORBIS, p. 8 (bottom); © Barry King/WireImage/Getty Images, p. 9; © J. Vespa/WireImage/Getty Images, p. 10; RSA/ZOJ WENN Photos/Newscom, p. 11; Clint Brewer/Splash News/Newscom, p. 12 (top left); © Todd Williamson/WireImage/Getty Images, p. 12 (top right); © Kevin Winter/Getty Images, pp. 12 (bottom), 19, 29 (top center); Seth Poppel Yearbook Library, p. 14; TM & Copyright © 20th Century Fox Film Corp. All rights reserved/Courtesy Everett Collection, p. 15; © Dimension Films/Courtesy Everett Collection, p. 16; BEImages/Rex USA, p. 17; Alex J. Berliner/BEImages/Rex USA, p. 18 (top); © Frank Robichon/epa/CORBIS, p. 18 (bottom left); © Summit Entertainment/Entertainment Pictures/ZUMA Press, p. 18 (bottom right); © Kevin Mazur/TCA 2009/WireImage/Getty Images, p. 20 (top); © iStockphoto.com/EdStock, p. 20 (bottom); Imprint Entertainment/Maverick Films/Summit Entertainment/Newscom, p. 21 (top); © Todd Strand/Independent Picture Service, p. 21 (bottom); © Summit Entertainment/Photofest, p. 23; Bruce Talamon/© Lionsgate/Courtesy Everett Collection, p. 24 (top); PacificCoastNews/Newscom, p. 24 (bottom left); © Lionsgate/Courtesy Everett Collection, p. 25; © Chelsea Lauren/WireImage/Getty Images, pp. 26 (left), 28 (right); © Dominique Charriau/WireImage/Getty Images, p. 26 (right); Picture Perfect/Rex USA, p. 27; © Jason Merritt/Getty Images, p. 28 (top); © Steve Grantiz/WireImage/Getty Images, p. 28 (bottom); © Photo Works/Shutterstock.com, p. 29 (top left); © Gregg DeGuire/FilmMagic/Getty Images, p. 29 (right); © Dave M. Benett/Getty Images, p. 29 (bottom).

Front cover: © Jon Furniss/WireImage/Getty Images (left); © Jeff Kravitz/FilmMagic/Getty Images (right).
Back cover: © Chelsea Lauren/WireImage/Getty Images.

Main body text set in Shannon Std Book 12/18.
Typeface provided by Monotype Typography.